easy meals

pasta

p

This is a Parragon Publishing Book
This edition published in 2004

Parragon Publishing
Queen Street House
4 Queen Street
Bath BA1 1HE, UK

ISBN: 1-40541-511-8

Printed in China

Produced by The Bridgewater Book Company Ltd, Lewes, East Sussex, UK

Acknowledgements
Creative Director Terry Jeavons
Art Director Sarah Howerd
Editorial Director Fiona Biggs
Senior Editor Mark Truman
Editorial Assistants Simon Bailey, Tom Kitch
Page Make-up Sara Kidd

NOTES FOR THE READER

- This book uses both US and metric measurements. Follow the same units of
  measurement throughout; do not mix US and metric.
- All spoon measurements are level: teaspoons are assumed to be 5 ml, and tablespoons are assumed to be 15 ml.
- Cup measurements in this book are for American cups.
- Unless otherwise stated, milk is assumed to be whole milk, eggs and individual
  vegetables such as potatoes are medium-sized, and pepper is freshly ground
  black pepper.
- Recipes using raw or very lightly cooked eggs should be avoided by infants, the
  elderly, pregnant women, convalescents, and anyone suffering from an illness.
- Optional ingredients, variations or serving suggestions have not been included in
  the calculations.
- The times given are an approximate guide only. Preparation times differ according
  to the techniques used by different people, and the cooking times vary as a result
  of the type of oven used.

Contents

Introduction

For an easy meal, one of the most versatile ingredients is pasta. It comes in a vast range of shapes and sizes: shells, bows, twists, quills, tubes, sheets, long, thin spaghetti, and nests of ribbonlike tagliatelle. Adding eggs to the pasta dough turns it a rich yellow, whole-wheat flour makes a brown pasta, and egg pasta may be combined with pasta flavored with spinach and tomatoes to make *pasta tricolore*, tinted with the three colors of the Italian flag. Pasta colored with squid ink is a dramatic black. Pasta may be flavored with mushrooms and a variety of other ingredients.

Pasta is very quick and easy to cook. Dried pasta is usually ready after about 12 minutes of cooking, and fresh pasta takes less than half that time. It may be combined with an apparently limitless range of meats, fish, dairy products, herbs, spices, and vegetables, which may be served as a sauce with freshly boiled

guide to recipe key	
easy	Recipes are graded as follows: 1 pea—easy; 2 peas—very easy; 3 peas—extremely easy.
serves 4	Most of the recipes in this book serve four people. Simply halve the ingredients to serve two, taking care not to mix US and metric measurements.
15 minutes	Preparation time. Where recipes include a soaking time, this is listed separately: e.g., 15 minutes, plus 30 minutes to soak.
15 minutes	Cooking time. Cooking times do not include the cooking of potatoes served with the main dishes.

pasta, or mixed into a pasta sauce. Pasta in a sauce may also be baked in the oven until golden brown. It is very tempting this way and children really enjoy dishes such as Casserole of Fusilli & Smoked Haddock, and Baked Cheese & Tomato Macaroni, a tasty variation of macaroni cheese.

Pasta dishes can be elegant. Veal Cutlets with Mascarpone & Marille, and Chicken & Wild Mushroom Lasagna are dishes for a special occasion. Spaghetti with Smoked Salmon is impressive and quick to make — salmon is folded into a cream sauce laced with whisky or brandy to add a touch of luxury.

Fideua, page 60

Soups

Pasta is very good for making a hearty soup. The classic pasta soups, Minestrone and Pistou, are packed with vegetables and small pasta shapes, and need only some fresh Parmesan cheese and a chunk of bread to make a light but satisfying one-dish meal. Pasta can be used to great visual effect in soups. Tiny pasta stars add to the appeal of Chicken Soup with Stars, a simple soup composed of chicken pieces in a well-flavored bouillon. Italian Fish Soup is a tasty version of an old favorite, and Potato and Parsley Soup with Pesto has an intriguing combination of flavors.

Chicken Soup with Stars

2¾ oz/75 g small pasta stars, or other very small shapes
chopped fresh parsley

CHICKEN BOUILLON
2 lb 12 oz/1.25 kg chicken pieces, such as wings or legs
10 cups water
1 stick of celery, sliced
1 large carrot, sliced
1 onion, sliced
1 leek, sliced
2 garlic cloves, crushed
8 peppercorns
4 allspice berries
3–4 parsley stems
2–3 fresh thyme sprigs
1 bay leaf
½ tsp salt
black pepper

❶ Begin by making the chicken bouillon. Put the chicken in a large 16 cup pot with the water, celery, carrot, onion, leek, garlic, peppercorns, allspice, herbs, and salt. Bring just to a boil and skim off the foam that rises to the surface. Reduce the heat and simmer, partially covered, for 2 hours.

❷ Remove the chicken from the bouillon and set aside to cool. Continue simmering the bouillon, uncovered, for about 30 minutes. When the chicken is cool enough to handle, remove the meat from the bones and, if necessary, cut into bite-size pieces.

❸ Strain the bouillon and remove as much fat as possible. Discard the vegetables and flavorings. (There should be about 7½ cups of chicken bouillon.)

❹ Bring the bouillon to a boil in a clean pan. Add the pasta and regulate the heat so that the bouillon boils very gently. Cook for about 10 minutes, or until the pasta is tender but still al dente, or firm to the bite.

❺ Stir in the chicken meat. Taste the soup and adjust the seasoning. Ladle the soup into warm bowls and serve at once, sprinkled with parsley.

very easy

serves 4

10–15 minutes

3 hours

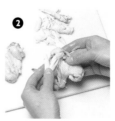

Minestrone

INGREDIENTS

1 tbsp olive oil
1 onion, chopped finely
1 leek, halved lengthwise
   and sliced thinly
2 garlic cloves,
   chopped finely
14 oz/400 g canned
   chopped tomatoes
   in juice
1 carrot, diced finely
1 small turnip,
   diced finely
1 small potato,
   diced finely
4½ oz/125 g peeled
   celery root, diced
   finely
9 oz/250 g peeled
   pumpkin, diced finely
3 cups water
4 cups chicken or
   vegetable bouillon
14 oz/400 g canned
   cannellini or borlotti
   beans, rinsed
3½ oz/100 g leafy
   cabbage
3 oz/85 g small pasta
   shapes or broken
   spaghetti
salt and pepper
freshly grated Parmesan
   cheese, to serve

❶ Heat the oil in a large pan over a medium heat. Add the onion, leek, and garlic, and cook for 3–4 minutes, stirring occasionally, until slightly softened.

❷ Add the tomatoes, carrot, turnip, potato, celery root, pumpkin, water, and bouillon. Bring to a boil, stirring occasionally.

❸ Stir in the beans and cabbage. Season lightly with salt and pepper. Reduce the heat and simmer, partially covered, for about 50 minutes, or until all the vegetables are tender.

❹ Bring plenty of salted water to a boil in a pan. Add the pasta and cook until it is just tender. Drain the pasta, then add it to the soup.

❺ Taste the soup and adjust the seasoning. Ladle at once into warm bowls and serve with Parmesan cheese to sprinkle on top.

extremely easy

serves 4

20 minutes

1 hour,
10 minutes

Pistou

INGREDIENTS

2 young carrots
2 potatoes
7 oz/200 g fresh peas
in the shells
7 oz/200 g thin green
beans
5½ oz/150 g young
zucchini
2 tbsp olive oil
1 garlic clove, crushed
1 large onion, chopped
finely
10 cups vegetable
bouillon or water
1 bouquet garni of
2 sprigs fresh parsley
and 1 bay leaf tied in
a 3 inch/7.5 cm piece
of celery
3 oz/85 g dried small
soup pasta
1 large tomato, skinned,
seeded, and chopped
or diced
pared Parmesan cheese,
to serve

PISTOU SAUCE
1½ cups fresh basil
leaves
1 garlic clove
5 tbsp fruity extra-virgin
olive oil
salt and pepper

 very easy

 serves 4

20 minutes

30 minutes

❶ To make the pistou sauce, put the basil leaves, garlic, and olive oil in a food processor and process until well blended. Season with salt and pepper to taste. Transfer to a bowl, then cover and chill until required.

❷ Peel the carrots and cut them in half lengthwise, then slice. Peel the potatoes and cut into fourths lengthwise, then slice. Set aside.

❸ Shell the peas. Trim the beans and cut them into 1 inch/2.5 cm pieces. Cut the zucchini in half lengthwise, then slice. Set aside.

❹ Heat the oil in a large pan or a flameproof casserole dish. Add the garlic and fry for 2 minutes, stirring. Add the onion and continue panfrying for 2 minutes, or until soft. Add the carrots and potatoes and stir for about 30 seconds.

❺ Pour in the bouillon and bring to a boil. Lower the heat, then partially cover the pan and simmer for 8 minutes, or until the vegetables start to become tender.

❻ Stir in the peas, beans, zucchini, bouquet garni, and pasta. Season, and cook for 4 minutes, or until the vegetables and pasta are tender. Stir in the pistou sauce and serve with Parmesan cheese parings.

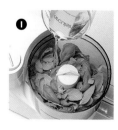

Italian Cream of Tomato Soup

INGREDIENTS

4 tbsp unsalted butter
1 large onion, chopped
2½ cups vegetable
   bouillon
2 lb/900 g Italian plum
   tomatoes, skinned
   and chopped roughly
pinch of baking soda
2 cups dried fusilli
1 tbsp superfine sugar
⅔ cup heavy cream
salt and pepper
fresh basil leaves,
   to garnish
deep-fried croûtons,
   to serve

❶ Melt the butter in a large pan, then add the onion, and fry for 3 minutes. Add 1¼ cups of vegetable bouillon to the pan, with the chopped tomatoes and baking soda. Bring the soup to a boil and simmer for 20 minutes.

❷ Remove the pan from the heat and set aside to cool. Purée the soup in a blender or a food processor and pour through a fine strainer back into the pan.

❸ Add the remaining vegetable bouillon and the fusilli to the pan, and season to taste with salt and pepper.

❹ Add the sugar to the pan and bring to a boil, then lower the heat and simmer for about 15 minutes.

❺ Pour the soup into a warm tureen and swirl the heavy cream around the surface of the soup, then garnish with fresh basil leaves. Serve immediately with deep-fried croûtons to sprinkle on top.

very easy

serves 4

15 minutes

1 hour

Potato & Parsley Soup with Pesto

3 strips rindless,
   smoked, fatty bacon
1 lb/450 g floury
   potatoes
1 lb/450 g onions
2 tbsp butter
2½ cups chicken bouillon
2½ cups milk
¾ cup dried conchigliette
⅔ cup heavy cream
chopped fresh parsley
salt and black pepper
freshly grated Parmesan
   cheese and garlic
   bread, to serve

PESTO SAUCE
1 cup finely chopped
   fresh parsley
2 garlic cloves, crushed
⅔ cup pine nuts, crushed
2 tbsp chopped fresh
   basil leaves
⅔ cup freshly grated
   Parmesan cheese
white pepper
⅔ cup olive oil

❶ To make the pesto sauce, put all of the ingredients in a blender or a food processor and process for 2 minutes, or blend together by hand.

❷ Chop the bacon, potatoes, and onions finely. Cook the bacon in a large pan over a medium heat for 4 minutes. Add the butter, potatoes, and onions, and cook for 12 minutes, stirring constantly.

❸ Add the bouillon and milk to the pan, then bring to a boil and simmer for 10 minutes. Add the conchigliette and simmer for another 12–14 minutes.

❹ Blend in the cream and simmer for 5 minutes. Add the parsley and 2 tablespoons of pesto sauce, and season with salt and black pepper. Transfer the soup to serving bowls and serve with grated Parmesan cheese and garlic bread.

 very easy

 serves 4

25 minutes

1 hour

Italian Fish Soup

INGREDIENTS

4 tbsp butter
1 lb/450 g assorted fish
    fillets, such as sea
    bass and snapper
1 lb/450 g prepared
    seafood, such as
    squid and shrimp
225 g/8 oz fresh
    crabmeat
1 large onion, sliced
¼ cup all-purpose flour
5 cups fish bouillon
¾ cup dried pasta
    shapes, such as
    ditalini or elbow
    macaroni
1 tbsp anchovy paste
grated zest and juice
    of 1 orange
¼ cup dry sherry
1¼ cups heavy cream
salt and black pepper
crusty brown bread,
    to serve

❶ Melt the butter in a large pan and add the fish fillets, seafood, crabmeat, and onion, then cook gently over a low heat for 6 minutes.

❷ Add the flour to the mixture, stirring thoroughly to prevent lumps from forming.

❸ Gradually add the fish bouillon, stirring constantly, until the soup comes to a boil. Reduce the heat and simmer the soup for 30 minutes.

❹ Add the pasta to the pan and cook for an additional 10 minutes, until it is tender but al dente, or firm to the bite.

❺ Stir in the anchovy paste, the orange zest and orange juice, and the sherry and heavy cream. Season to taste with salt and pepper.

❻ Heat the soup until it is completely warmed through. Transfer the soup to a tureen or to warm soup bowls and serve hot with crusty brown bread.

 extremely easy

serves 4

5 minutes

 1 hour

Main Meals

Tasty sauces of ground meat cooked with tomatoes form the basis for many classic pasta recipes. One dish that never seems to lose its popularity is Spaghetti Bolognese. The recipe in this section is made extra special by the addition of chicken livers, prosciutto, and rich Marsala wine. Spaghetti is tossed in a tomato and anchovy sauce for Pasta Puttanesca, a dish given extra texture by the addition of chopped olives and capers. Classic Italian meatballs are casseroled in an Oyster, Mushroom & Wine Sauce.

Big Pot of Simmered Meat

INGREDIENTS

4 lb 8 oz/2 kg beef, pork, chicken for stewing — any combination or just one type
2 onions, chopped
1 whole garlic bulb, divided into cloves and peeled
several sprigs of fresh herbs, such as parsley, oregano, and cilantro
1 carrot, sliced
1–2 bouillon cubes
salt and pepper
cooked macaroni or thin noodles, to serve
finely sliced scallions, to garnish

❶ Place the meat in a large pan and cover with cold water. Bring to a boil and skim off the scum that forms on the surface. Reduce the heat and add the onions, garlic, herbs, and carrot. Simmer, covered, for 1 hour.

❷ Add the bouillon cubes and salt and pepper to taste. (If using a combination of meat and chicken, cook the meat first for 1 hour, then add the chicken.) Continue to simmer over a very low heat for about 2 hours, or until the meat is very tender.

❸ Remove from the heat and let the meat cool in the bouillon. Using a slotted spoon, transfer the meat to a board and shred; set aside. Skim the fat from the bouillon, or let chill, then remove the fat by lifting it off. Strain the soup to clarify it. Reheat before serving.

❹ To serve, spoon the hot macaroni or noodles into soup bowls, then top with the shredded meat and ladle the soup over the top. Garnish with scallions and serve.

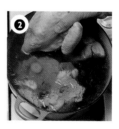

 easy

 serves 4

 20 minutes

 3½ hours, plus 1 hour to cool

Garlic-Flavored Chicken Cushions

4 part-boned chicken
   halves
½ cup frozen spinach,
   defrosted
½ cup ricotta cheese
2 garlic cloves, crushed
1 tbsp olive oil
1 onion, chopped
1 red bell pepper, sliced
14 oz/400 g canned
   chopped tomatoes
6 tbsp wine or chicken
   bouillon
10 stuffed olives, sliced
salt and pepper
pasta, to serve

❶ Make a slit between the skin and meat on one side of each chicken half. Lift the skin to form a pocket, taking care to leave the skin attached to the other side.

❷ Put the spinach into a strainer and press out the water with a spoon. Mix with the ricotta, half the garlic, and the seasoning. Spoon the mixture under the skin of each chicken half, then secure the edge of the skin with toothpicks.

❸ Heat the oil in a skillet, then add the onion and cook for 1 minute, stirring. Add the remaining garlic and red bell pepper, and cook for 2 minutes. Stir in the tomatoes, wine or bouillon, olives, and seasoning. Set the sauce aside and chill the chicken if preparing in advance.

❹ Bring the sauce to a boil, then pour into a shallow heat-resistant dish and arrange the chicken halves on top in a single layer.

❺ Cook, uncovered, in a preheated oven, 400°F/200°C, for 35 minutes, or until the chicken is golden and cooked through. Test by making a slit in one of the chicken halves with a skewer to make sure the juices run clear and not pink. Spoon a little of the sauce over the chicken halves, then transfer to warm serving plates. Serve with pasta.

 easy

 serves 4

20 minutes

 40 minutes

❶

❷

❹

24

Spaghetti Bolognese

INGREDIENTS

3 tbsp olive oil
2 garlic cloves, crushed
1 large onion,
    chopped finely
1 carrot, diced
2 cups lean ground beef,
    veal, or chicken
3 oz/85 g chicken livers,
    chopped finely
3½ oz/100 g lean
    prosciutto, diced
⅔ cup Marsala wine
10 oz/280 g canned
    chopped
    plum tomatoes
1 tbsp chopped fresh
    basil leaves
2 tbsp tomato paste
salt and pepper
1 lb/450 g dried
    spaghetti

❶ Heat 2 tablespoons of the olive oil in a large pan, then add the garlic, onion, and carrot, and panfry for 6 minutes.

❷ Add the ground beef, veal, or chicken, the chicken livers, and the prosciutto to the pan, and cook over a medium heat for 12 minutes, or until well browned.

❸ Stir in the Marsala wine, tomatoes, basil, and tomato paste, and cook for 4 minutes. Season to taste with salt and pepper. Cover the pan, and simmer for 30 minutes.

❹ Remove the lid from the pan and stir the meat and vegetables, then simmer for another 15 minutes.

❺ Meanwhile, bring a large pan of lightly salted water to a boil. Add the spaghetti and the remaining oil, and cook for about 12 minutes, or until tender but still firm to the bite. Drain and transfer to a serving dish. Pour the sauce over the pasta and toss gently together, then serve.

extremely easy

serves 4

15 minutes

1 hour,
10 minutes

26

Meatballs in an Oyster, Mushroom & Wine Sauce

INGREDIENTS

2 cups white bread
    crumbs
⅔ cup milk
2 tbsp butter
9 tbsp olive oil
3 cups sliced
    oyster mushrooms
¼ cup whole-wheat flour
⅞ cup beef bouillon
⅔ cup red wine
4 tomatoes, skinned
    and chopped
1 tbsp tomato paste
1 tsp brown sugar
1 tbsp finely chopped
    fresh basil
12 shallots, chopped
4 cups ground steak
1 tsp paprika
1 lb/450 g dried egg
    tagliarini pasta
salt and pepper
fresh basil sprigs,
    to garnish

❶ Soak the bread crumbs in the milk for 30 minutes.

❷ Heat half the butter and 4 tablespoons of the oil in a pan. Cook the mushrooms for 4 minutes, then stir in the flour and cook for 2 minutes. Add the bouillon and wine and simmer for 15 minutes. Add the tomatoes, tomato paste, sugar, and basil. Season well and simmer for 30 minutes.

❸ Mix the shallots, steak, and paprika with the bread crumbs and season. Shape the mixture into 14 meatballs.

❹ Heat 4 tablespoons of the remaining oil and the remaining butter in a large skillet. Cook the meatballs, turning frequently, until brown all over. Transfer to a deep casserole and pour over the red wine and the mushroom sauce, then cover and bake in a preheated oven at 350°F/180°C for 30 minutes.

❺ Bring a pan of salted water to a boil. Add the pasta and the remaining oil and cook until tender. Drain and transfer to a serving dish. Remove the casserole from the oven and cool for 3 minutes. Pour the meatballs and sauce onto the pasta, then garnish with the basil sprigs and serve.

easy

serves 4

25 minutes,
plus 30 minutes
to soak

1¾ hours

Sicilian Spaghetti

²⁄₃ cup olive oil, plus
  extra for brushing
2 eggplants
3 cups ground beef
1 onion, chopped
2 garlic cloves, crushed
2 tbsp tomato paste
14 oz/400 g canned
  chopped tomatoes
1 tsp Worcestershire
  sauce
1 tsp chopped fresh
  marjoram or oregano
  or ½ tsp dried
  marjoram or oregano
½ cup pitted black olives,
  sliced
1 green, red, or yellow
  bell pepper, cored,
  seeded, and chopped
6 oz/175 g dried
  spaghetti
1 cup freshly grated
  Parmesan cheese
salt and pepper
fresh oregano or parsley
  sprigs, to garnish

❶ Brush an 8 inch/20 cm loose-based round cake pan with oil, line the base with baking parchment, and brush with oil.

❷ Slice the eggplants. Heat a little oil in a skillet and cook the eggplants in batches until browned on both sides. Add more oil, as necessary. Drain on paper towels.

❸ Put the beef, onion, and garlic in a pan, and cook over a medium heat, stirring, until browned. Add the tomato paste, tomatoes, Worcestershire sauce, marjoram or oregano, and salt and pepper. Simmer for 10 minutes, stirring from time to time. Add the olives and bell pepper and panfry for another 10 minutes.

❹ Bring a pan of salted water to a boil. Add the spaghetti and 1 tablespoon of olive oil, and cook until tender but still firm to the bite. Drain and turn the spaghetti into a bowl. Add the meat mixture and cheese, and toss with 2 forks.

❺ Arrange eggplant slices over the base and up the sides of the pan. Add the spaghetti and then cover with the rest of the eggplant slices. Bake in a preheated oven at 400°F/200°C for 40 minutes. Let stand for 5 minutes, then invert onto a serving dish. Discard the baking parchment. Garnish with sprigs of fresh oregano or parsley, and serve the pasta dish at once, piping hot.

 easy

 serves 4

 20 minutes

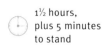 1½ hours, plus 5 minutes to stand

Lasagna Verde

INGREDIENTS

butter, for greasing
14 sheets precooked
  lasagna
3¾ cups béchamel sauce
¾ cup grated
  mozzarella cheese
fresh basil (optional),
  to garnish

MEAT SAUCE
2 tbsps olive oil
4 cups ground beef
1 large onion, chopped
1 celery stalk, diced
4 cloves garlic, crushed
¼ cup all-purpose flour
1¼ cups beef bouillon
⅔ cup red wine
1 tbsp chopped fresh
  parsley
1 tsp chopped fresh
  marjoram
1 tsp chopped fresh basil
2 tbsp tomato paste
salt and pepper

❶ To make the meat sauce, heat the olive oil in a large skillet. Add the ground beef and panfry, stirring frequently, until browned all over. Add the onion, celery, and garlic, and cook for 3 minutes.

❷ Sprinkle the flour over the beef and continue to panfry, stirring constantly, for 1 minute. Stir in the bouillon and red wine a little at a time, season well with salt and pepper, and add the parsley, marjoram, and basil. Bring to a boil, then lower the heat, and simmer for 35 minutes. Add the tomato paste and simmer for another 10 minutes.

❸ Grease an ovenproof dish lightly with butter. Arrange sheets of lasagna over the base of the dish and spoon a layer of meat sauce, then béchamel sauce over the top. Place another layer of lasagna on top and repeat the process twice, finishing with a layer of béchamel sauce. Sprinkle the grated mozzarella cheese over the top.

❹ Bake the lasagna in a preheated oven at 375°F/190°C for 35 minutes, or until the top is golden brown and bubbling. Serve immediately while the top is bubbling, perhaps garnished with chopped fresh basil.

 easy

 serves 4

 15 minutes

 1¾ hours

Pasticcio

INGREDIENTS

2 cups dried fusilli
1 tbsp olive oil, plus
    extra for brushing
4 tbsp heavy cream
salt
fresh rosemary sprigs,
    to garnish
mixed salad, to serve

SAUCE
2 tbsp olive oil
1 onion, sliced thinly
1 red bell pepper, cored,
    seeded, and chopped
2 garlic cloves, chopped
5¼ cups ground beef
14 oz/400 g canned
    chopped tomatoes
½ cup dry white wine
2 tbsp chopped fresh
    parsley
2¼ oz/60 g canned
    anchovies, drained
    and chopped
salt and pepper

TOPPING
1¼ cups plain yogurt
3 eggs
pinch of freshly grated
    nutmeg
⅓ cup freshly grated
    Parmesan cheese

easy

serves 4

15 minutes

1 hour

❶ To make the sauce, heat the oil in a skillet and panfry the onion and red bell pepper for 3 minutes. Add the garlic and cook for 1 minute. Add the beef and cook until browned.

❷ Add the tomatoes and wine to the pan and bring to a boil. Lower the heat and simmer for 20 minutes, or until thickened. Stir in the parsley and anchovies, and season to taste with salt and pepper.

❸ Bring a pan of salted water to a boil. Add the pasta and oil and cook for 10 minutes, or until almost tender. Drain and transfer to a bowl. Stir in the cream.

❹ For the topping, beat the yogurt, eggs, and nutmeg.

❺ Brush an ovenproof dish with oil. Spoon in half the pasta and cover with half the meat sauce. Repeat, then spread the topping over the meat sauce and sprinkle with cheese.

❻ Bake in a preheated oven at 375°F/190°C for 25 minutes, or until golden. Garnish the dish with rosemary and serve it piping hot with a mixed salad.

Veal Cutlets with Mascarpone & Marille

INGREDIENTS

⅞ cup butter
4 x 9 oz/250 g veal
*   cutlets, trimmed*
1 large onion, sliced
2 apples, peeled, cored,
*   and sliced*
6 oz/175 g white
*   mushrooms*
1 tbsp chopped fresh
*   tarragon*
8 black peppercorns
1 tbsp sesame seeds
14 oz/400 g dried
*   marille pasta*
scant ½ cup extra-virgin
*   olive oil*
¾ cup mascarpone
*   cheese, broken into*
*   small pieces*
2 large beefsteak
*   tomatoes, cut in half*
leaves of 1 fresh
*   basil sprig*
salt and pepper
fresh basil leaves,
*   to garnish*

❶ Melt 4 tablespoons of butter in a skillet. Cook the veal over a low heat for 5 minutes on each side. Transfer to a dish and keep warm.

❷ Cook the onion and apples in the pan till lightly browned. Transfer to a dish, put the veal on top, and keep warm.

❸ Melt the remaining butter in the skillet. Cook the mushrooms, tarragon, and peppercorns gently over a low heat for 3 minutes. Sprinkle the sesame seeds over the top.

❹ Bring a pan of salted water to a boil. Add the pasta and 1 tablespoon of the oil. Cook until tender but still firm to the bite. Drain and transfer to a serving plate.

❺ Top the pasta with the mascarpone cheese and sprinkle the remaining olive oil over it. Place the onions, apples, and veal cutlets on top of the pasta. Spoon the mushrooms, peppercorns, and pan juices onto the cutlets, arrange the tomatoes and basil leaves around the edge, and bake in a preheated oven at 300°F/150°C for 5 minutes.

❻ Season to taste with salt and pepper, then garnish with fresh basil leaves, and serve immediately.

easy

serves 4

15 minutes

about 30 minutes

Stuffed Cannelloni

INGREDIENTS

8 dried cannelloni tubes
1 tbsp olive oil
¼ cup freshly grated
    Parmesan cheese
fresh herb sprigs,
    to garnish

STUFFING

2 tbsp butter
10½ oz/300 g frozen
    spinach, thawed
    and chopped
½ cup ricotta cheese
¼ cup freshly grated
    Parmesan cheese
¼ cup chopped ham
pinch of freshly grated
    nutmeg
2 tbsp heavy cream
2 eggs, beaten lightly
salt and pepper

SAUCE

2 tbsp butter
¼ cup all-purpose flour
1¼ cups milk
2 bay leaves
pinch of freshly grated
    nutmeg

❶ To make the stuffing, melt the butter in a pan and stir-fry the spinach for 2–3 minutes. Remove from the heat and stir in the ricotta and Parmesan cheeses and the ham. Season with nutmeg, salt, and pepper. Beat in the cream and eggs to make a thick paste.

❷ Bring a pan of lightly salted water to a boil. Add the pasta and the oil, and simmer for 10–12 minutes, or until almost tender. Drain and set aside to cool.

❸ To make the sauce, melt the butter in a pan. Stir in the flour and cook, stirring, for 1 minute. Stir in the milk a little at a time. Add the bay leaves and simmer, stirring, for about 5 minutes, then add the nutmeg, salt, and pepper. Remove from the heat and discard the bay leaves.

❹ Spoon the filling into a piping bag and fill the cannelloni.

❺ Spoon a little sauce into the base of an ovenproof dish. Arrange the cannelloni in the dish in a single layer and pour the remaining sauce over the top. Sprinkle the Parmesan cheese over the top and bake the cannelloni in a preheated oven at 375°F/190°C for 40–45 minutes. Garnish with fresh herb sprigs and serve.

 easy

 serves 4

 20 minutes

 1 hour,
plus 10 minutes
to cool

Whole-Wheat Spaghetti with Suprêmes of Chicken

INGREDIENTS

⅛ cup canola oil
3 tbsp olive oil
4 x 8 oz/225 g chicken
   suprêmes
⅔ cup orange brandy
2 tbsp all-purpose flour
⅔ cup freshly squeezed
   orange juice
1 oz/25 g zucchini, cut
   into short, thin sticks
1 oz/25 g red bell
   pepper, cut into short,
   thin sticks
1 oz/25 g leek, finely
   shredded
14 oz/400 g dried whole-
   wheat spaghetti
3 large oranges, peeled
   and cut into segments
zest of 1 orange, cut into
   very fine strips
2 tbsp chopped fresh
   tarragon
⅔ cup ricotta cheese
salt and pepper
fresh tarragon leaves,
   to garnish

❶ Heat the canola oil and 1 tablespoon of the olive oil in a skillet. Add the chicken and panfry until golden brown. Add the orange brandy and cook for 3 minutes more. Sprinkle the flour over the top and cook for 2 minutes.

❷ Lower the heat and add the orange juice, zucchini, bell pepper, and leek, and season. Simmer for 5 minutes, or until the sauce has thickened.

❸ Meanwhile, bring a pan of salted water to a boil. Add the spaghetti and 1 tablespoon of the olive oil and cook for 10 minutes. Drain, then transfer to a serving dish, and drizzle the remaining oil over the top.

❹ Add half the orange segments, half the orange zest, the tarragon, and the ricotta cheese to the sauce in the skillet, and cook for 3 minutes.

❺ Place the chicken on top of the pasta and pour a little sauce over the top, then garnish with the remaining orange segments and zest, and the tarragon. Serve immediately.

very easy

serves 4

15 minutes

about 30 minutes

Chicken & Wild Mushroom Lasagna

butter, for greasing
14 sheets precooked
   lasagna
3½ cups béchamel sauce
¾ cup grated Parmesan
   cheese

CHICKEN & WILD
MUSHROOM SAUCE
2 tbsp olive oil
2 garlic cloves, crushed
1 large onion, chopped
   finely
8 oz/225 g wild
   mushrooms, sliced
2½ cups ground chicken
3 oz/85 g chicken livers,
   chopped finely
4 oz/115 g prosciutto,
   diced
⅔ cup Marsala wine
10 oz/280 g canned
   chopped tomatoes
1 tbsp chopped fresh
   basil leaves
2 tbsp tomato paste
salt and pepper

❶ To make chicken and wild mushroom sauce, heat the olive oil in a large pan. Add the garlic and onion, and the mushrooms, and panfry, stirring frequently, for 6 minutes.

❷ Add the ground chicken, chicken livers, and prosciutto, and cook over a low heat for 12 minutes, or until the meat has browned.

❸ Stir the Marsala wine, tomatoes, basil, and tomato paste into the mixture in the pan, and cook for 4 minutes. Season to taste with salt and pepper, cover, and simmer for about 30 minutes. Uncover the pan and stir, then simmer for an additional 15 minutes.

❹ Grease an ovenproof dish lightly with butter. Arrange sheets of lasagna over the base of the dish and spoon a layer of chicken and wild mushroom sauce over them, then spoon a layer of béchamel sauce over the top. Place another layer of lasagna on top and repeat the process twice, finishing with a layer of béchamel sauce. Sprinkle grated cheese over the top and bake in a preheated oven at 375°F/190°C for 35 minutes, or until golden brown and bubbling. Serve immediately.

easy

serves 4

20 minutes

1¾ hours

Sliced Duckling with Linguine

INGREDIENTS

4 x 9½ oz/275 g boned
   halves of duckling
2 tbsp butter
⅓ cup finely chopped
   carrots
4 tbsp finely chopped
   shallots
1 tbsp lemon juice
⅔ cup meat bouillon
4 tbsp clear honey
¾ cup fresh raspberries,
   or thawed frozen
   raspberries
¼ cup all-purpose flour
1 tbsp Worcestershire
   sauce
14 oz/400 g fresh
   linguine
1 tbsp olive oil
salt and pepper

TO GARNISH
fresh raspberries
fresh sprig of flatleaf
   parsley

❶ Trim and score the duck halves with a sharp knife, and season them well all over. Melt the butter in a skillet, then add the duck halves, and cook all over until lightly colored.

❷ Add the carrots, shallots, lemon juice, and half the meat bouillon, and simmer over a low heat for 1 minute. Stir in half the honey and half the raspberries. Sprinkle half the flour over the mixture and cook, stirring, for 3 minutes. Season with pepper and add the Worcestershire sauce.

❸ Stir in the remaining bouillon and cook for 1 minute. Stir in the remaining honey and raspberries and sprinkle the remaining flour over the top. Cook for another 3 minutes.

❹ Remove the duck halves from the pan, but let the sauce continue simmering over a very low heat.

❺ Meanwhile, bring a large pan of lightly salted water to a boil. Add the linguine and olive oil, and cook until tender but still firm to the bite. Drain and divide between 4 individual plates.

❻ Slice the duck half lengthwise into ¼ inch/5 mm thick pieces. Pour a little sauce over the pasta and arrange the sliced duck in a fan shape on top of it. Garnish with raspberries and flatleaf parsley, and serve immediately.

 very easy

 serves 4

 10 minutes

20 minutes

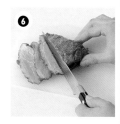

Pasta with Broccoli & Anchovy Sauce

INGREDIENTS

1 lb 2 oz/500 g broccoli
14 oz/400 g dried
  orecchiette
5 tbsp olive oil
2 large garlic cloves,
  crushed
1¾ oz/50 g canned
  anchovy fillets in oil,
  drained and
  chopped finely
2¼ oz/60 g Parmesan
  cheese, grated finely
2¼ oz/60 g romano
  cheese, grated finely
salt and pepper

very easy

serves 4

10 minutes

15 minutes

❶ Bring 2 pans of lightly salted water to a boil. Chop the broccoli florets and stems into small, bite-size pieces. Add the broccoli to one pan and cook until very tender. Drain and set aside.

❷ Put the pasta in the other pan of boiling water and cook for 10–12 minutes, or according to the instructions on the package, until al dente, or firm to the bite.

❸ Meanwhile, heat the olive oil in a large pan over a medium heat. Add the garlic and cook for 3 minutes, stirring, without letting it brown. Add the chopped anchovies to the oil and cook for 3 minutes, stirring and mashing with a wooden spoon to break them up.

❹ Drain the pasta, add it to the pan of anchovies and stir gently. Add the broccoli and continue stirring to mix the ingredients well.

❺ Add the grated Parmesan and romano cheeses to the pasta and stir constantly over medium–high heat until the cheeses melt and the pasta and broccoli are coated.

❻ Adjust the seasoning to taste—the anchovies and cheeses are salty, so you will just need to add pepper, if anything. Spoon into bowls or onto plates, and serve at once.

COOK'S TIP

If orecchiette, the small, shell-shaped pasta, is hard to find, substitute pasta bows.

Spaghetti with Corsican Clam Sauce

INGREDIENTS

14 oz/400 g fresh or
  dried spaghetti
salt and pepper

CORSICAN CLAM
SAUCE
2 lb/900 g clams in
  their shells
4 tbsp olive oil
3 large garlic cloves,
  crushed
pinch of dried chili flakes
  (optional)
2 lb/900 g tomatoes,
  skinned and chopped,
  with juice reserved
2¼ oz/60 g green or
  black olives, pitted
  and chopped
1 tbsp chopped fresh
  oregano, or
  ½ tsp dried oregano

❶ Begin by making the clam sauce. Rinse the clams under cold, running water and scrub them lightly to remove any sand from the shells. Discard any broken clams or open clams that do not shut when firmly tapped with the back of a knife. This indicates they are dead and could cause food poisoning if eaten. Let the clams soak in a large bowl of water for about 30 minutes. Meanwhile, bring a large pan of lightly salted water to a boil.

❷ Heat the oil in a large skillet over a medium heat. Add the garlic and chili flakes, if using, and panfry for 2 minutes. Stir in the tomatoes, olives, and oregano. Lower the heat and simmer, stirring frequently, until the tomatoes soften and start to break up. Cover the pan and simmer for 10 minutes.

❸ Meanwhile, cook the spaghetti in the pan of boiling water according to the instructions on the package until just al dente. Drain well, reserving about ½ cup of the cooking water. Keep the pasta warm.

❹ Add the clams and reserved cooking liquid to the sauce, and stir. Bring to a boil, stirring. Discard any clams that do not open and transfer the rest to a larger pan.

❺ Add the pasta to the sauce and toss until well coated. Transfer it to individual dishes and serve at once.

easy

serves 4

10 minutes,
plus 30 minutes
to soak

15 minutes

Pasta with Tuna & Lemon

INGREDIENTS

4 tbsp butter, diced
1¼ cups heavy cream
4 tbsp lemon juice
1 tbsp grated lemon zest
½ tsp anchovy paste
14 oz/400 g dried fusilli
7 oz/200 g canned tuna
   in olive oil, drained
   and flaked
salt and pepper

TO GARNISH
2 tbsp finely chopped
   fresh parsley
grated lemon zest

❶ Bring a large pan of lightly salted water to a boil. Melt the butter in a large skillet. Stir in the heavy cream and lemon juice, and let simmer, for about 2 minutes, or until slightly thickened, stirring frequently.

❷ Stir in the lemon zest and anchovy paste. Meanwhile, cook the pasta for 10–12 minutes, or according to the instructions on the package, until just al dente. Drain well.

❸ Add the sauce to the pasta and toss until well coated. Add the tuna and toss gently until well blended but not too broken up.

❹ Season to taste with salt and pepper. Transfer to a serving plate and garnish with the parsley and lemon zest. Grind black pepper over the pasta and serve at once.

extremely easy

serves 4

5 minutes

15 minutes

COOK'S TIP
As an alternative, use the thin, twist-shaped pasta casareccie.

Pasta Puttanesca

3 tbsp extra-virgin
  olive oil
1 large red onion,
  chopped finely
4 anchovy fillets, drained
pinch of chili flakes
2 garlic cloves,
  chopped finely
14 oz/400 g canned
  chopped tomatoes
2 tbsp tomato paste
8 oz/225 g dried
  spaghetti
½ cup pitted black olives,
  chopped roughly
½ cup pitted green
  olives, chopped
  roughly
1 tbsp capers, drained
  and rinsed
4 sun-dried tomatoes,
  chopped roughly
salt and pepper

❶ Heat the oil in a pan and add the onion, anchovies, and chili flakes. Cook for 10 minutes until softened and starting to brown. Add the garlic and cook for 30 seconds.

❷ Add the tomatoes and tomato paste and bring to a boil. Simmer gently for 10 minutes.

❸ Meanwhile, cook the spaghetti in plenty of boiling salted water according to the package instructions, or until tender but still firm to the bite.

❹ Add the olives, capers, and sun-dried tomatoes to the sauce. Simmer for another 2–3 minutes. Season to taste.

❺ Drain the pasta well and stir the sauce carefully into it. Toss well to mix thoroughly. Serve immediately.

extremely easy

serves 4

10 minutes

about 30 minutes

Seafood Lasagna

¼ cup butter
6 tbsp all-purpose flour
1 tsp mustard powder
2½ cups milk
2 tbsp olive oil
1 onion, chopped
2 garlic cloves, chopped
   finely
1 tbsp fresh thyme leaves
3 cups mixed
   mushrooms, sliced
⅔ cup white wine
14 oz/400 g canned
   chopped tomatoes
1 lb/450 g mixed skinless
   white fish fillets,
   cubed
8 oz/225 g fresh
   scallops, trimmed
4–6 sheets fresh lasagna
8 oz/225 g mozzarella
   cheese, drained and
   chopped
salt and pepper

❶ Melt the butter in a pan. Add the flour and mustard powder, and stir until smooth. Simmer gently for 2 minutes without coloring. Add the milk little by little, whisking until smooth. Bring to a boil and simmer for 2 minutes. Remove from the heat and set aside. Cover the surface of the sauce with plastic wrap to prevent a skin forming.

❷ Heat the oil in a skillet and add the onion, garlic, and thyme. Cook gently for 5 minutes, or until softened. Add the mushrooms and cook for another 5 minutes, or until softened. Stir in the wine and boil rapidly until nearly evaporated. Stir in the tomatoes. Bring to a boil and simmer, covered, for 15 minutes. Season and set aside.

❸ Grease a lasagna dish lightly. Spoon half the tomato sauce into the dish and top with half the fish and scallops.

❹ Layer half the lasagna over the fish and pour half the white sauce over it. Then sprinkle half the mozzarella cheese on top. Repeat these two layers, finishing with a top layer of white sauce and mozzarella cheese.

❺ Place in a preheated oven, 400°F/200°C, and bake for 35–40 minutes, or until the top is bubbling and golden and the fish cooked through. Remove from the oven and let stand for 10 minutes before serving.

easy

serves 4

25 minutes

1¼ hours,
plus 10 minutes
to stand

Linguine with Sardines

8 sardines, filleted
1 bulb fennel
4 tbsp olive oil
3 garlic cloves, sliced
1 tsp chili flakes
12 oz/350 g dried
   linguine
½ tsp finely grated
   lemon zest
1 tbsp lemon juice
2 tbsp pine nuts, toasted
2 tbsp chopped fresh
   parsley
salt and pepper

 extremely easy

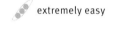 serves 4

 10 minutes

 15 minutes

COOK'S TIP
Reserve a couple of
tablespoons of the
pasta cooking water
and add to the pasta
with the sauce if the
mixture seems a
little dry.

❶ Wash and dry the sardine fillets, then chop them roughly into large pieces and set aside. Trim the fennel bulb and slice very thinly.

❷ Heat 2 tablespoons of the olive oil in a large skillet and add the garlic and chili flakes. Cook for 1 minute, then add the fennel. Cook over a medium–high heat for 4–5 minutes, or until softened. Add the sardine pieces and cook for another 3–4 minutes, or until just cooked.

❸ Meanwhile, cook the pasta in plenty of boiling salted water, or according to the package instructions, until tender but still firm to the bite. Drain well and return to the pan.

❹ Add the lemon zest, lemon juice, pine nuts, parsley, and seasonings to the sardines, and toss together. Add to the linguine with the remaining olive oil and toss them gently. Serve immediately while the pasta is still hot, garnished with a sprinkling of parsley.

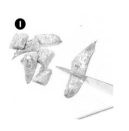

Spaghettini with Crab

 extremely easy

 serves 4

 15 minutes

15 minutes

❶ Scoop the meat from the crab shell into a bowl. Mix the white and brown meat lightly together and set aside.

❷ Bring a large pan of salted water to a boil and add the spaghettini. Cook according to the instructions on the package, or until tender but still firm to the bite. Drain well and return to the pan.

❸ Meanwhile, heat 2 tablespoons of the olive oil in a skillet. When hot, add the chile and garlic. Stir-fry them for 30 seconds before adding the crab meat, parsley, lemon juice, and lemon zest. Stir-fry for another minute until the crab is just heated through.

❹ Add the crab mixture to the pasta with the remaining olive oil and seasoning. Toss together thoroughly and serve immediately, garnished with lemon wedges.

COOK'S TIP
As an alternative to a dressed crab, use a large fresh crab weighing about 2 lb 4 oz/1 kg.

Fideua

INGREDIENTS

3 tbsp olive oil
1 large onion, chopped
2 garlic cloves, chopped
  finely
pinch of saffron, crushed
½ tsp paprika
3 tomatoes, skinned,
  seeded, and chopped
12 oz/350 g Spanish
  fideos, or egg
  vermicelli, broken into
  2 inch/5 cm lengths
⅔ cup white wine
1¼ cups fish bouillon
12 large raw jumbo
  shrimp
18 live mussels,
  scrubbed and bearded
12 oz/350 g cleaned
  squid, cut into rings
18 large clams, scrubbed
2 tbsp chopped fresh
  parsley
salt and pepper
lemon wedges, to serve

❶ Heat the oil in a large skillet or a paella pan. Add the onion and cook gently for 5 minutes, or until softened. Add the garlic and cook for another 30 seconds. Add the saffron and paprika and stir well. Add the tomatoes and panfry for an additional 2–3 minutes, or until they have collapsed.

❷ Add the vermicelli and stir well. Add the wine and boil rapidly until absorbed.

❸ Add the fish bouillon, shrimp, mussels, squid, and clams. Stir and return to a low simmer for 10 minutes, or until the shrimp and squid are cooked through and the mussels and clams have opened. The bouillon should be almost completely absorbed.

❹ Add the parsley and season to taste. Serve immediately in warm bowls, garnished with lemon wedges.

 very easy

 serves 4

 20 minutes

 30 minutes

Sea Bass with Olive Sauce on Macaroni

INGREDIENTS

1 lb/450 g dried
macaroni
1 tbsp olive oil
8 x 4 oz/115 g sea bass
medallions

TO GARNISH
lemon slices
shredded leek
shredded carrot

OLIVE SAUCE
2 tbsp butter
4 shallots, chopped
2 tbsp capers
1½ cups pitted green
olives, chopped
4 tbsp balsamic vinegar
1¼ cups fish bouillon
1¼ cups heavy cream
juice of 1 lemon
salt and pepper

❶ To make the sauce, first melt the butter in a skillet. Add the shallots and panfry them over a low heat for 4 minutes to soften them. Add the capers and olives and cook them for an additional 3 minutes.

❷ Stir in the balsamic vinegar and fish bouillon, then bring to a boil and reduce by half. Add the cream, stirring, and reduce again by half. Season to taste with salt and pepper and stir in the lemon juice. Remove the pan from the heat and set it aside, keeping it warm.

❸ Bring a pan of salted water to a boil. Add the pasta and olive oil, and cook for 12 minutes, or until just al dente.

❹ Meanwhile, place the sea bass medallions in a broiling pan and broil them lightly for 3–4 minutes on each side, or until cooked through, but still moist and delicate.

❺ Drain the macaroni thoroughly and transfer it to large individual serving dishes. Top the pasta with the fish medallions and pour the olive sauce over them. Garnish with lemon slices, shredded leek, and shredded carrot, and serve immediately while still hot.

 easy

 serves 4

 10 minutes

 30 minutes

Casserole of Fusilli & Smoked Haddock

INGREDIENTS

2 tbsp butter, plus extra
  for greasing
1 lb/450 g smoked
  haddock fillets,
  cut into 4 slices
2½ cups milk
¼ cup all-purpose flour
pinch of freshly grated
  nutmeg
3 tbsp heavy cream
1 tbsp chopped fresh
  parsley
2 eggs, hard cooked and
  mashed to a pulp
4 cups dried fusilli
1 tbsp lemon juice
salt and pepper
flatleaf parsley leaves,
  to garnish
boiled new potatoes and
  beet, to serve

❶ Grease a casserole with butter. Put the haddock in the casserole and pour the milk over it. Place the dish in a preheated oven at 400°F/200°C, and bake the haddock for about 15 minutes. Pour the cooking liquid carefully into a pitcher without breaking up the fish.

❷ Melt the butter in a pan and stir in the flour. Whisk in the reserved cooking liquid a little at a time. Season to taste with salt, pepper, and nutmeg. Stir in the cream, parsley, and mashed egg, and simmer in the pan, stirring constantly, for about 2 minutes.

❸ Meanwhile, bring a large pan of lightly salted water to a boil. Add the fusilli and lemon juice, and simmer until the fusilli is tender but still firm to the bite.

❹ Drain the pasta and spoon or tip it over the fish. Pour the egg sauce over the pasta. Return the casserole to the oven and bake for 10 minutes.

❺ Serve the casserole straight from the oven, garnished with flatleaf parsley, with boiled new potatoes and beet.

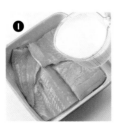

 easy

 serves 4

 10 minutes

35 minutes

Vegetarian Light Meals

Pasta, vegetables, and herbs make an excellent combination for light meals. Paglia e Fieno (green and white pasta with peas) and Green Tagliatelle with Garlic are examples of the superb, simple, tasty dishes at which Italian cooks excel. Spinach & Wild Mushroom Lasagna is an imaginative version of the classic baked pasta dish. Tagliatelle with Pumpkin includes prosciutto in its unusual cream sauce, and Spaghetti with Smoked Salmon is one of the popular light fish dishes included in this section.

Spinach & Herb Orzo

INGREDIENTS

1 tsp salt
9 oz/250 g dried orzo
  pasta
7 oz/200 g baby spinach
  leaves
5½ oz/150 g arugula
1 oz/25 g fresh flatleaf
  parsley leaves
1 oz/25 g fresh cilantro
  leaves
4 scallions
2 tbsp extra-virgin
  olive oil
1 tbsp garlic-flavored
  olive oil
pepper

TO SERVE
radicchio or other lettuce
  leaves
2¼ oz/60 g feta cheese,
  well drained and
  crumbled (optional)
lemon slices

❶ Bring 2 pans of water to a boil, and put 12 ice cubes in a bowl of cold water. Add the salt and orzo pasta to one pan, then return it to a boil and cook the pasta for 8–10 minutes, or according to package instructions, until it is tender.

❷ Meanwhile, remove the spinach stems if they are tough. Rinse the leaves in several changes of water to remove any grit. Chop the arugula, parsley, cilantro, and green parts of the scallions roughly.

❸ Put the spinach, arugula, parsley, cilantro, and scallions in the other pan of boiling water and blanch them for 15 seconds. Drain and transfer the greens to the iced water to preserve their color.

❹ When the spinach, herbs, and scallions are cool, squeeze out all the excess water. Transfer to a food processor, and process. Add the olive oil and garlic-flavored oil, and process again until well blended.

❺ Drain the orzo well and tip it into a bowl. Stir in the spinach mixture, toss well, and adjust the seasoning.

❻ Line a plate with radicchio leaves and pile the orzo on top. Sprinkle with feta cheese, if desired, and garnish with lemon slices. Serve hot or let cool to room temperature.

easy

serves 4

15 minutes

10 minutes

Dry Soup of Thin Noodles

INGREDIENTS

12 oz/350 g very thin
pasta, such as fideos
or capellini

2–3 bay leaves

2–3 chorizo sausages

1 onion, chopped

1 green bell pepper or
mild green chile,
such as anaheim or
poblano, seeded
and chopped

4–5 garlic cloves,
chopped finely

1½ cups strained
tomatoes

1½ cups hot chicken,
meat, or vegetable
bouillon

¼ tsp ground cumin

½ tsp mild red chili
powder

pinch of dried oregano
leaves

12 oz/350 g grated
sharp cheese

2 tbsp chopped fresh
cilantro

❶ Boil the pasta in boiling salted water with the bay leaves. Drain and discard the bay leaves. Rinse the noodles to rid them of excess starch, and let drain.

❷ Panfry the chorizo in a skillet. As soon as it begins to brown, add the chopped onion, bell pepper, and garlic, then continue panfrying, stirring the pan occasionally, until all the vegetables are softened.

❸ Add the strained tomatoes, bouillon, cumin, chili, and oregano, and remove the pan from the heat.

❹ Toss the pasta with the hot sauce, then transfer to an ovenproof dish. Level the surface with a spoon, then cover the mixture with a layer of the grated cheese.

❺ Bake the pasta in a preheated oven at 400°F/200°C for about 15 minutes, or until the top is lightly browned and the pasta is heated through. Serve at once, sprinkled with the chopped fresh cilantro.

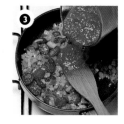

 very easy

 serves 4

 10 minutes

25 minutes

Spaghetti alla Carbonara

INGREDIENTS

15 oz/425 g dried
   spaghetti
2 tbsp olive oil
1 large onion, sliced
   thinly
2 garlic cloves, chopped
6 oz/175 g rindless
   bacon, cut into
   thin strips
2 tbsp butter
6 oz/175 g mushrooms,
   sliced thinly
1¼ cups heavy cream
3 eggs, beaten
scant 1 cup freshly grated
   Parmesan cheese,
   plus extra to serve
   (optional)
salt and pepper
fresh sage sprigs,
   to garnish

❶ Warm a large serving dish or bowl. Bring a large pan of lightly salted water to a boil. Add the spaghetti to the pan with 1 tablespoon of the oil, and cook until tender but still al dente. Drain, return to the pan, and keep warm.

❷ Meanwhile, heat the remaining oil in a skillet over a medium heat. Add the onion and cook until it is transparent. Add the garlic and bacon, and panfry until the bacon is crisp. Transfer to the warm plate.

❸ Melt the butter in the skillet. Add the mushrooms and panfry, stirring occasionally, for 3–4 minutes. Return the bacon mixture to the pan. Cover and keep warm.

❹ Mix together the cream, eggs, and cheese in a large bowl and then season to taste with salt and pepper.

❺ Working very quickly, tip the spaghetti into the bacon and mushroom mixture, and pour the eggs over them. Toss the spaghetti quickly into the egg and cream mixture, using 2 forks, and serve immediately, garnished with sprigs of sage and extra grated Parmesan cheese.

 very easy

 serves 4

15 minutes

15 minutes

Tagliatelle with Pumpkin

INGREDIENTS

INGREDIENTS

1 lb 2 oz/500 g pumpkin
   or butternut squash,
   peeled
3 tbsp olive oil
1 onion, chopped finely
2 garlic cloves, crushed
4–6 tbsp chopped fresh
   parsley
pinch of freshly grated
   nutmeg
about 1 cup chicken or
   vegetable bouillon
4 oz/115 g prosciutto
9 oz/250 g dried
   tagliatelle
²⁄₃ cup heavy cream
salt and pepper
freshly grated Parmesan
   cheese, to serve

❶ Cut the pumpkin or butternut squash in half and scoop out the seeds with a spoon. Cut the pumpkin or squash into ½ inch/1 cm dice.

❷ Heat 2 tablespoons of the olive oil in a large pan. Add the onion and garlic and cook over a low heat for 3 minutes, or until softened. Add half the parsley and cook for 1 minute.

❸ Add the pumpkin or squash pieces and panfry for 2–3 minutes. Season to taste with salt, pepper, and nutmeg.

❹ Add half the bouillon to the pan and bring to a boil, then cover and simmer for about 10 minutes, or until the pumpkin or squash is tender. Add more bouillon if the vegetables are drying out and likely to burn.

❺ Add the prosciutto to the pan and cook, stirring frequently, for another 2 minutes.

❻ Meanwhile, bring a pan of salted water to a boil. Add the tagliatelle and the remaining oil, and cook for 12 minutes, or until tender. Drain and transfer to a warm serving dish.

❼ Stir the cream into the pumpkin and ham mixture, then heat it through and spoon the mixture over the pasta. Sprinkle the remaining parsley over the top, and serve at once. Hand the grated Parmesan cheese round separately.

very easy

serves 4

15 minutes

35 minutes

Spaghetti al Tonno

INGREDIENTS

7 oz/200 g canned tuna,
  drained
2¼ oz/60 g canned
  anchovies, drained
1 cup olive oil
1 cup roughly chopped
  flatleaf parsley
⅔ cup lowfat cream or
  ricotta cheese
1 lb/450 g dried
  spaghetti
2 tbsp butter
salt and pepper
black olives, to garnish
crusty bread, to serve

❶ Remove any bones from the tuna. Put the fish into a food processor or a blender, with the anchovies, 1 cup of the olive oil, and the flatleaf parsley. Process until a smooth sauce is formed.

❷ Spoon the lowfat cream or ricotta cheese into the food processor or blender, and process again for a few seconds to blend thoroughly. Season with salt and black pepper.

❸ Bring a large pan of lightly salted water to a boil. Add the spaghetti and the remaining olive oil, and cook until tender but still firm to the bite.

❹ Drain the spaghetti, then return it to the pan and place over a medium heat. Add the butter and toss well to coat the pasta thoroughly. Spoon in the sauce and quickly toss into the spaghetti, using 2 forks.

❺ Remove the pan from the heat and divide the spaghetti between 4 warm individual serving plates. Garnish with the olives and serve immediately with warm, crusty bread.

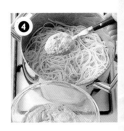

extremely easy

serves 4

5 minutes

10–12 minutes

Spaghetti with Smoked Salmon

INGREDIENTS

1 lb/450 g dried
   buckwheat spaghetti
2 tbsp olive oil
½ cup crumbled feta
   cheese
salt
fresh cilantro or parsley
   leaves, to garnish

SAUCE
1¼ cups heavy cream
⅔ cup whisky or brandy
4½ oz/125 g smoked
   salmon
pinch of cayenne pepper
black pepper
2 tbsp chopped fresh
   cilantro or parsley

❶ Bring a large pan of lightly salted water to a boil. Add the spaghetti and 1 tablespoon of the olive oil, and cook until tender but still firm to the bite. Drain the spaghetti, then return to the pan, and sprinkle the remaining olive oil over it. Cover the pan and shake it, set it aside and keep it warm.

❷ To make the sauce, pour the cream into a small pan and bring it to simmering point. Pour the whisky or brandy into another small pan and bring it to simmering point. Remove both pans from the heat, without letting either boil, and mix together the cream and whisky or brandy.

❸ Cut the smoked salmon into thin strips and add to the cream mixture. Season to taste with cayenne and black pepper. Just before serving, stir in the chopped fresh cilantro or parsley.

❹ Transfer the spaghetti to a warm serving dish, then pour the sauce over the top and toss thoroughly with 2 large forks. Scatter the crumbled feta cheese on top, garnish with the cilantro or parsley leaves, and serve immediately.

 very easy

 serves 4

 5 minutes

10–12 minutes

Macaroni & Shrimp Bake

INGREDIENTS

3 cups dried short-cut macaroni
1 tbsp olive oil, plus extra for brushing
6 tbsp butter, plus extra for greasing
2 small fennel bulbs, sliced thinly and fronds reserved
6 oz/175 g mushrooms, sliced thinly
6 oz/175 g shelled, cooked shrimp
pinch of cayenne pepper
1¼ cups béchamel sauce
⅔ cup freshly grated Parmesan cheese
2 large tomatoes, sliced
1 tsp dried oregano
salt and pepper

❶ Bring a pan of salted water to a boil. Add the pasta and oil, and cook until tender but still firm to the bite. Drain and return to the pan. Add 2 tablespoons of butter, then cover and shake the pan, and set it aside, keeping it warm.

❷ Melt the remaining butter in a pan and cook the fennel for 3–4 minutes. Stir in the mushrooms and cook for 2 minutes. Stir in the shrimp, then remove the pan from the heat.

❸ Stir the cayenne pepper and shrimp mixture into the béchamel sauce, then toss the sauce into the pasta. Spoon the mixture into a greased ovenproof dish and spread evenly. Sprinkle the Parmesan cheese on top and arrange the tomato slices in a ring around the edge. Brush them with olive oil and sprinkle the oregano over the dish.

❹ Bake in a preheated oven at 350°F/180°C for 25 minutes, or until golden brown. Serve immediately.

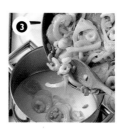

 easy

 serves 4

15 minutes

40 minutes

80

Paglia e Fieno

INGREDIENTS

4 tbsp butter
2 lb/900 g fresh peas,
   shelled
⅞ cup heavy cream
1 lb/450 g mixed fresh
   green and white
   spaghetti or tagliatelle
1 tbsp olive oil
⅔ cup freshly grated
   Parmesan cheese,
   plus extra to serve
pinch of freshly grated
   nutmeg
salt and pepper

❶ Melt the butter in a large pan. Add the peas and cook over a low heat for 2–3 minutes.

❷ Using a measuring pitcher, pour ⅔ cup of the cream into the pan and bring to a boil, then simmer for 1–1½ minutes, or until slightly thickened. Remove the pan from the heat.

❸ Meanwhile, bring a large pan of lightly salted water to a boil. Add the spaghetti or tagliatelle and olive oil, and cook for 2–3 minutes, or until just tender but still al dente. Remove the pan from the heat, drain the pasta thoroughly, and return it to the pan.

❹ Add the peas and cream sauce to the pasta. Return the pan to the heat and add the remaining cream and the Parmesan cheese. Season to taste with salt, black pepper, and grated nutmeg.

❺ Using 2 forks, toss the pasta gently to coat it with the peas and cream sauce while it heats through.

❻ Transfer the pasta to a serving dish and serve at once, with extra Parmesan cheese handed round separately.

very easy

serves 4

10 minutes

12 minutes

Green Tagliatelle with Garlic

INGREDIENTS

2 tbsp walnut oil
1 bunch scallions, sliced
2 garlic cloves,
    sliced thinly
3¼ cups sliced
    mushrooms
1 lb/450 g fresh green
    and white tagliatelle
1 tbsp olive oil
8 oz/225 g frozen
    spinach, thawed
    and drained
½ cup soft cheese with
    garlic and herbs
4 tbsp light cream
½ cup chopped, unsalted
    pistachio nuts
salt and pepper

TO GARNISH
2 tbsp shredded
    fresh basil
fresh basil sprigs
Italian bread, to serve

❶ Heat the walnut oil in a large skillet. Add the scallions and garlic, and cook for 1 minute, or until just softened.

❷ Add the mushrooms to the pan, stir well, cover, and panfry over a low heat for 5 minutes, or until they are soft.

❸ Meanwhile, bring a large pan of lightly salted water to a boil. Add the tagliatelle and olive oil to the pan, and simmer for 3–5 minutes, or until tender but still firm to the bite. Drain the tagliatelle thoroughly and return to the pan.

❹ Add the spinach to the skillet and cook it for 1–2 minutes to heat it through. Add the cheese to the pan and let it melt slightly. Stir the cream into the spinach and cheese, and continue to cook, without letting the mixture come to a boil, until warmed through.

❺ Pour the sauce over the pasta, then season to taste with salt and black pepper and mix well. Heat through gently, stirring constantly, for 2–3 minutes.

❻ Transfer the pasta and sauce mixture to a serving dish and sprinkle the pistachio nuts over the top with the shredded basil. Garnish the pasta with the basil sprigs, and serve it immediately with an Italian bread of your choice and perhaps a fresh salad.

 very easy

 serves 4

10 minutes

15 minutes

Spinach & Wild Mushroom Lasagna

INGREDIENTS

½ cup butter, plus extra
for greasing
2 garlic cloves,
chopped finely
4 oz/115 g shallots
8 oz/225 g wild
mushrooms, such
as chanterelles
1 lb/450 g spinach,
cooked, drained, and
chopped finely
2 cups grated
Cheddar cheese
¼ tsp freshly grated
nutmeg
1 tsp chopped fresh basil
2¼ oz/60 g all-purpose
flour
2½ cups hot milk
⅔ cup grated Cheshire
cheese
salt and pepper
8 sheets precooked
lasagna
fresh baby spinach
leaves, to garnish

❶ Grease an ovenproof dish lightly with a little butter.

❷ Melt 4 tablespoons of the butter in a pan. Add the garlic, shallots, and wild mushrooms, and panfry them over a low heat for 3 minutes. Stir in the spinach, Cheddar cheese, nutmeg, and basil. Season well with salt and pepper, and set the pan aside.

❸ Melt the remaining butter in another pan over a low heat. Add the flour and cook, stirring constantly, for 1 minute. Stir in the hot milk a little at a time, whisking constantly until smooth. Stir in ¼ cup of the Cheshire cheese and season to taste with salt and pepper.

❹ Spread half the mushroom and spinach mixture over the base of the prepared dish. Cover with a layer of lasagna and half the cheese sauce. Repeat the layering and sprinkle the remaining Cheshire cheese on top. Bake in a preheated oven at 400°F/200°C for 30 minutes, or until golden. Serve straight from the oven, garnished with baby spinach leaves.

 easy

 serves 4

 15 minutes

45 minutes

Vegetable Lasagna

1 eggplant, sliced
3 tbsp olive oil
2 garlic cloves, crushed
1 red onion, sliced
1 green bell pepper, diced
1 red bell pepper, diced
1 yellow bell pepper,
  diced
8 oz/225 g mixed
  mushrooms, sliced
2 celery stalks, sliced
1 zucchini, diced
½ tsp chili powder
½ tsp ground cumin
2 tomatoes, chopped
1¼ cups strained tomato
2 tbsp chopped basil
8 sheets no precook
  lasagna verde
salt and pepper

CHEESE SAUCE
2 tbsp butter or
  margarine
1 tbsp flour
⅔ cup vegetable
  bouillon
1¼ cups milk
¾ cup Cheddar cheese,
  grated
1 tsp Dijon mustard
1 tbsp chopped basil
1 egg, beaten

❶ Place the eggplant in a colander, sprinkle with salt, and let stand for 20 minutes. Rinse in cold water, drain and reserve.

❷ Heat the oil in a pan and sauté the garlic and onion for 1–2 minutes. Add the bell peppers, mushrooms, celery, and zucchini, and cook for 3–4 minutes, stirring. Stir in the spices and cook for 1 minute. Mix the tomatoes, strained tomatoes, and basil together, and season well.

❸ To make the sauce, melt the butter in a pan, add the flour and cook for 1 minute. Remove from the heat and stir in the bouillon and milk. Return to the heat and add half of the cheese and the mustard. Boil, stirring, until thick. Stir in the basil, and season. Remove from the heat and stir in the egg.

❹ Line an ovenproof dish with half the lasagna. Cover with half the vegetables, then with the tomato sauce, then with a layer of eggplants. Repeat, then spoon the sauce on top. Sprinkle with cheese and cook in a preheated oven, 350°F/180°C, for 40 minutes. Serve immediately.

 easy

serves 4

 30 minutes

about 1 hour

Baked Cheese & Tomato Macaroni

INGREDIENTS

2 cups elbow macaroni
1½ cups grated
    vegetarian cheese
scant 1 cup grated
    Parmesan cheese
4 tbsp fresh white bread
    crumbs
1 tbsp chopped basil
1 tbsp butter or
    margarine

TOMATO SAUCE
1 tbsp olive oil
1 shallot, chopped finely
2 garlic cloves, crushed
1 lb/450 g canned
    chopped tomatoes
1 tbsp chopped basil
salt and pepper

❶ To make the tomato sauce, heat the oil in a pan and sauté the shallots and garlic for 1 minute. Add the tomatoes, basil, and salt and pepper to taste, then cook over a medium heat, stirring, for 10 minutes.

❷ Meanwhile, cook the macaroni in a pan of boiling salted water for 8 minutes, or until just undercooked. Drain.

❸ Mix both of the cheeses together in a dish.

❹ Grease a deep ovenproof dish. Spoon one third of the tomato sauce into the base of the dish and top with one third of the macaroni and then one third of the cheeses. Season with salt and pepper. Repeat the layers twice.

❺ Combine the bread crumbs and basil, and sprinkle over the top. Dot with the butter or margarine and cook in a preheated oven, 375°F/190°C, for 25 minutes, or until the dish is golden brown and bubbling. Serve.

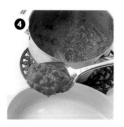

 easy

 serves 4

15 minutes

40 minutes

Olive, Bell Pepper & Cherry Tomato Pasta

INGREDIENTS

2 cups penne
2 tbsp olive oil
2 tbsp butter
2 garlic cloves, crushed
1 green bell pepper,
*   sliced thinly*
1 yellow bell pepper,
*   sliced thinly*
16 cherry tomatoes,
*   halved*
1 tbsp chopped oregano
½ cup dry white wine
2 tbsp pitted black
*   olives, cut into fourths*
2¾ oz/75 g arugula
salt and pepper
fresh oregano sprigs,
*   to garnish*

❶ Cook the pasta in a pan of boiling salted water for 8–10 minutes or until al dente. Drain thoroughly.

❷ Heat the oil and butter in a pan until the butter melts. Sauté the garlic for 30 seconds. Add the bell peppers and cook for 3–4 minutes, stirring.

❸ Stir in the cherry tomatoes, oregano, wine, and olives. Cook for 3–4 minutes. Season well with salt and pepper and stir in the arugula until just wilted.

❹ Transfer the pasta to a serving dish, spoon the sauce over it, and mix well. Garnish with oregano, and serve.

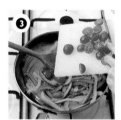

extremely easy

serves 4

10 minutes

10 minutes

COOK'S TIP

Make sure the pan is large enough to prevent the pasta from sticking together while cooking.

Spinach & Pine Nut Pasta

8 oz/225 g pasta shapes, or spaghetti
½ cup olive oil
2 garlic cloves, crushed
1 onion, sliced and cut into fourths
3 large flat mushrooms, sliced
8 oz/225 g spinach
2 tbsp pine nuts
6 tbsp dry white wine
salt and pepper
Parmesan shavings, to garnish

❶ Cook the pasta in a pan of boiling salted water for 8–10 minutes or until al dente. Drain well.

❷ Meanwhile, heat the oil in a large pan and sauté the garlic and onion for 1 minute.

❸ Add the sliced mushrooms and cook for 2 minutes, stirring occasionally.

❹ Add the spinach and cook for 4–5 minutes, or until the leaves have wilted.

❺ Stir in the pine nuts and wine, then season well and cook for 1 minute.

❻ Transfer the pasta to a warm serving bowl. Spoon the vegetable mixture into it and mix it into the pasta. Garnish with shavings of Parmesan cheese and serve at once.

 extremely easy

serves 4

5–10 minutes

12 minutes

 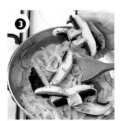 

COOK'S TIP

Nutmeg blends well with spinach, so grate a little over the dish just before serving to give it extra flavor.